The Holiday Cycle

The Holiday Cycle

poems by Joseph Mills

Press 53

Winston-Salem

Press 53, LLC
PO Box 30314
Winston-Salem, NC 27130

First Edition

Cover art, "Ghost in Brown Field," by Monstera Production.
Free use through Pexels.com

Library of Congress Control Number
2025931277

ISBN 978-1-950413-93-5

To My Family: Cookie King Champions all

Contents

New Year's Day

She says it's stupid
to begin the year here.
It makes no sense
solar or season-wise.
More logical would be
starting at an equinox,
the first day of spring,
Christmas day, the birth
of Muhammad or Buddha,
even National Donut Day,
honoring that sweet circle.

He says rules and rituals
are arbitrary. We are
born when we are born,
then tell ourselves
it means something
about fate, knowing
it's not true, or true only
in retrospect, the way
a tornado is measured
by the destruction it does.
That's why he refuses
to make resolutions.

She shrugs and says
she has an aunt who refuses
to take baths. To her,
making resolutions is like
when an optometrist asks,
"Which lens is better? This?
or This? This? Or this?"
They are a way of trying
to bring our blurred selves

back into focus, to remember
who it is we want to be and
how it is we want to live.

I want to be younger, he says.
I should make a resolution,
she says, to try not to smack you
this year. He says, Do or do not.
There is no try. She says, Ah,
May the Fourth. That would be
a good day to start the year.

The Gifts

On birthdays, holidays and visits,
my mother always gave blankets,
fuzzy ones, wool ones, fleeces,
throws, afghans, quilts, comforters,

each time saying something like
"You can keep it in your trunk," or
"It can go on your couch" or simply
"I just thought you could use it,"

and my father liked to give flashlights,
camping lights, outdoor strings,
solar pen lights to clip to keychains,
lamps he'd made in his workshop,

and I would give a sarcastic "Thanks.
Just what I needed," and put them aside.
It would be years before I understood
these gifts, my parents, warmth and light.

Snow Day

Before the weather channel began showing us the future,
some mornings you would wake to unexpected snow
and a cancelled school day. Once I spent such a holiday
sledding and skating, and, when I finally went home,
I was freezing. After his factory shift, my father came
to my bedroom to say goodnight and found me shivering.
He stood in the dark, rubbing my legs until I was warm.
Years later, when I had children of my own, I realized
how tired he must have been, how he must have known
his dinner was growing cold and his drink warm.
I have forgotten much of my schooling, but not those
snow day lessons: how joy can arrive unexpectedly,
how pleasure has its dangers, how love can be difficult
to forecast, its accumulation clear only in retrospect.

On the Way Home from the Civil Rights Museum My Fourteen-Year-Old Daughter Explains Why She Wants to Get a Tattoo

... they only knew it was Emmett Till
because of the ring he was wearing...

Groundhog Day

Each year I'm sure I've gotten it wrong.
Why would a sunny day in February mean
more winter is on the way? Just as I never
remember if I'm supposed to feed a fever
and starve a cold or vice versa. I know
there is wisdom among the animals
and in old folk lore sayings and practices—
hospitals are even bringing back leeches—
but it's perverse to pretend a rodent knows
our future when for decades we've ignored
the data showing the earth is warming.

Groundhogs only live around six years,
so Punxsutawney Phil died long long ago,
yet still we applaud this magical marmot,
this wonderous whistlepig, this variation
of Persephone, Eastre, Christ. Phil Is Dead!
Long Live Phil! Who among us doesn't want
to believe in rebirth, reincarnation, resurrection?
And, if a phoenix rising from the flames seems
a little too on point, why not a pudgy pugbelly?

We turn away from inconvenient truths
to shop. We buy another fan. We watch
the Bill Murray movie again. We continue
to celebrate the woodchuck as prophet,
not because we want to know the future,
because we want to believe we have one.

Super Bowl Sunday

In the future, people may not know what football was,
but they will continue to celebrate Super Bowl Sunday.
They will gather to feast, dressing in oversized jerseys
and tribal colors. They'll pass sacred objects around,
engage in ancient folk dances like The Wave, and sing
"Hubba Hubbba Hike!" and "Touch Up! Touch Down!"
"Did You Know?" features will explain the day's origin—
how families would set out giant or "super" bowls of food
as offerings to the gods of good fortune. Academics will
detail how city-states built coliseums as forums to pit sects
against one another, Patriots versus Saints versus Vikings,
or to stage animal-baitings of Bears, Panthers, Dolphins.
Religious groups and atheists will denounce the day,
but they'll find it as unstoppable as Santa's sleigh.
Most won't care about origins; they'll simply respond
to the power of gathering together, the pleasure of goals
and rituals, however inexplicable, the warmth of being
a body huddling among other bodies, the comfort
of a time out on the dark journey through winter.

Because He's Still Recuperating His Partner Makes the Annual Happy Birthday Darwin! Cake

A couple weeks after the surgery,
he finally can sit outside,
under the enormous black walnut tree
that hasn't yet succumbed to a storm
although it loses limbs each time.
In his lap he holds a biography
of Gregor Mendel, the monk
who cross-bred plants
and discovered genetic inheritance.

At one point, he had thought about
the church as a career. His mother had
suggested it would be a good place
for someone with his "proclivities,"
a comment so complicated he kept
returning to the statement for years
trying to determine if it was caring,
Machiavellian or something else.
He had studied science instead,
dedicating himself to Darwin.

She doesn't know he's been sick.
They haven't talked since the wedding
when the state finally allowed him
and Greg to be a legal couple,
and yet, this was when
his grandmother began talking
openly to him about relationships
in the months before her death.
Some things skip a generation.
Some things never get passed down.

He sees Greg glancing out the window
and he holds up the book,
like a preacher with a bible,
waggling it to reassure his partner
he's okay, awake, breathing, alive.
Greg holds up a batter-slick spatula
and waggles it in return.

Valentine

In second grade, Mrs. Connor liked to use
the word "special." Things, people, places
were "special," but some, like the valentines
we made for her with construction paper,
were "especially special." These she displayed,
and it made us feel good about ourselves.

In high school, we would learn to mock people
who used phrases like that or "very unique."
We would argue about the difference between
flammable and inflammable, woke and awoke,
bone and debone, God and Satan, love and hate,
learning how to wield words as weapons,
and we were too smart and too cool to think
anything was special.

But some of us would return
one day to the pleasures of our younger selves,
the music and movies we had become embarrassed of.
We would become more forgiving and more willing
to accept that, yes, there are things and people
who are "especially special." Like who? Like
a woman who tries to teach young children how
with only crayons, colored paper, and effort,
they can make something that will touch others,
something extraordinary, even extra extraordinary.

What Love May Look Like

A pre-dawn interstate. A thermos of coffee.
Next to me, the boy spiraled into himself asleep.
He went to bed in his uniform to be ready
for the tournament, and I simply prodded him
from bed to van after carrying out his bag and cleats.
When he wakes, he'll groggily eat the breakfast
his mother made at midnight before going to bed.
She also is asleep, at home, farther and farther away.
When she wakes, she will prepare breakfast
for our other child. Neither will think to say thanks
this morning. Perhaps they never will. Or maybe,
as with me now, it will occur to them years later
after they too have stumbled through a dark house
trying to gather together what their children need.

What's Revealed

At 50, she had kept rescheduling her colonoscopy
because she was afraid. He said it would be a gift
to him since he wanted her around as long as possible,
and so she finally went in. Afterwards, they were told,
when the anesthesia began to hit, she had exclaimed,
"Oh. . . here I go. I'll see you later," and that on waking
she had been happy and laughing, wishing everyone
a Merry Christmas even though it was August. In contrast,
when he'd had his, he had awoken combative, saying,
"you sons of bitches, I'll get you." In the following years,
they had laughed at this at parties, suggesting it revealed
something fundamental about people. At the end, again
in a hospital, she had given him another gift, squeezing
his hand, and saying, "Oh. . . here I go. I'll see you later."

Anniversary

I ask where she wants to go,
and she says the Berkeley Hills,

that place we housesat for a week
the one with the view of the bay,

the hot tub, and the old green BMW
with the sticky manual transmission.

She wants to go back thirty years ago
to when we imagined it was possible

someday for us to live like that,
when we still didn't know where

our choices would lead, before
it became clear which would end

in heartache and exhaustion, before
the nights of broken glass. She wants

to go back to the possible, the feeling
of the possible, the hope. We know

we can't get there from here.
So what to say? That she is so

beautiful still? That even if we chose
differently, I would choose with her?

I say, yeah, that car was fun to drive.

Checkpoints

Gray-haired and gray-bearded, I stand
at the elementary school entrance waiting
for an administrator to escort me
to a class to give a writing workshop.
I watch the carpool line and remember
those years when gym shoes lit up and
backpacks were in the shape of animals.
Then my daughter texts "Good Morning!
"It's National Margarita Day!" She pins
several locations where I can go get one.

Our relationship has changed since
she turned twenty-one. On that day
I supposedly took her out for her "first drink"
although we both knew that was a lie.
I was tempted to get her a cheap whiskey,
a bitter beer, a sour ale she would dislike,
because I was afraid at the floodgates
of alcohol opening, but I've been scared
since her birth, one definition of love.
She ordered a piña colada then, and now
she sends signals off satellites about BOGOs
and Happy Hours. I respond to her text
with an emoji. I watch children and parents
arrive holding hands. I watch as they let go.

Marching Fourth

As the bong got passed around,
my housemate pointed out,
"This is the only day
that's a command,"
which seemed profound
as most things did
at those moments,
and then he did a pompous walk
around the kitchen
and we laughed as we did
at most things in those moments.

Decades later, I ask my children
"Do you know what day it is?"
then answer, "March Fourth!"
and parade step around.
They groan, return to eating,
and I think of how I learned
the joke from an old friend
who has children of his own now
and Parkinson's,
both of us transformed
from stoner lost boys to soccer dads,
that stereotypical joke
Time delights in telling
as it marches forth,
the one both stupid and profound.

Teaching My Son How to Spell F-O-R-N-I-C-A-T-I-O-N and Other Conversations

i.
My son has access to music more explicit
than anything I ever listened to at his age,
and when my wife and I ban certain songs,
he hears them anyway. At his friends' houses
or in public places like the gym or mall.
He doesn't understand most of the lyrics,
not just the double-entendres, but the words
themselves, "Ho," "bitch," "gold-digger."
We talk about misogyny and race and slurs,
the complex usage and history of words,
but it's too much for him. He just likes the beat.

ii.
My first month living in France,
when I knew little of the language
except for *Bonjour* and *Ça va?*
at a campus mixer, a girl taught me
to say, *Je suis monté comme un an,*
and I kept repeating the sentence,
liking how the words felt in my mouth
although they meant nothing to me.
I walked around the party, giddily,
saying loudly for everyone to hear,
"I am hung like a donkey."
"Hello. How are you?
I am hung like a donkey."

iii.
As we listen to the radio, my son asks,
"Is this song about sex too?" I say, "Yes,"
pointing out the rhyme "vacation/fornication."
He asks, "What's fornication?" I tell him,
and he wants to know how to spell it.
Later, he tells his mother, "I learned a new word.
Four Nations. It means sex. I can even spell it."
She says, "It's good to have a vocabulary."

iv.
When I was young, my family drove to Florida
to visit my grandmother who had moved
from Indiana to a trailer park in Bradenton,
and we had dinner at a seafood restaurant.
It was amazing. There were palm trees
in the parking lot. There was a dessert
called key-lime pie. There were even
vending machines in the bathroom.
I came back to the table and asked,
"Grandma, What's a French Tickler
and why do they come in different colors
and can I have some quarters to get one?"
Suddenly, there was an awkward silence
that I didn't understand for years, and
an anger that I still don't understand.

v.
As he clicks through radio stations,
my son announces, "I'm a version
although I won't be after I have sex,
which is weird because it sounds like
something you should be afterwards.
You should become a version."
I agree it's weird. He wants to know
if I'm a version. I tell him I'm not.
I wait, but he doesn't ask anything else.

Education

When my children began attending school,
I learned new holiday customs like how to put
ice in the toilet before bedtime to make it snow
or the need to wear green on March 17 to avoid
getting pinched. They told me how "wee ones"
turn over desks, and it was good luck to catch one
because then they have to grant three wishes,
so I found myself encouraging my children
in their attempts to try to trap and force a ransom
from a small enraged fearful stranger. Sometimes
as I helped them search for the right clothes to wear,
as we tried to master the charms and rituals
to protect against violence or lead to good fortune,
the radio would report on another school shooting,
making it clear how futile magical thinking can be
in this world. On the way to school we would talk
about what we would buy with a pot of gold.
I would say a tower to lock them in, a house of bricks,
maybe 365 toilets and an ice maker so it would snow
all the time and they'd never have to go to school.
They would say ice cream machines in their bedroom.

Archaeology

Some sounds would seem to have gone extinct,
the latch clank of your grandparents' 1940's fridge,
the scratch of a Red Devil match to light a pipe,
the backfiring of your uncle's Chevy station wagon,
the pumping to prime an old Coleman camping stove,
the rotary dial of a phone, a dial up modem connecting,
the woompfs as someone flips through albums quickly
like an experienced secretary at a filing cabinet,

then you discover a store with large bins of records
and, inside the door, you stop, close your eyes, and
listen to the sound of people browsing through jackets,
a collective whisper of searching, desire, and longing,
one you would put on your Golden Record to send out
to distant stars to give a sense of life on this planet.

And Also With You

When my son was young, I would tell him,
With great power comes great responsibility.
We didn't go to church, but he knew the story
of Spider-Man, and I hoped it might offer a code
to live by as his muscles and mind developed,

and then came another story and years
of light saber battles in the house and yard,
his difficulty at Halloween choosing between
being Darth Maul or Darth Vader, a choice
that probably should have given me pause,

and then the years of struggle trying to resist
the pull of darkness and to master the anger
as we played out an age-old generational story
of grievance and conflict, destruction and exile,
one that left us both wounded and scarred,

and now, as we try to build some sort of bridge
across the abyss between us, we sit and rewatch
Star Wars movies together because they provide
the comfort and calm of the familiar, like sports,
offering a shared experience outside of ourselves.

I'm annoyed anew by Jar Jar Binks and struck by
how whiny the young Luke Skywalker is, but it's
satisfying to eat popcorn and yell at the screen
until the moment I have forgotten or blocked—
Kylo Ren killing Han, the son killing the father.

These seductive stories we are raised on
—sons killed on crosses, fathers on crosswalks—
we may need to find other ones if we're to survive.
As we say goodnight, my son pauses and asks,
"Are you all right, Daddy?" a question and concern

he hasn't expressed for years. I say, "I am, or
I will be, I hope, and we know how important
hope is." He laughs. I say, "Maybe tomorrow
or soon we can start a new story." He says, "Okay,"
surprises me with a hug, and heads to his room.

Overheard at the Children's Museum

Would you please stop touching that?
I'm going to count to three.
When did you last have the hat?
If you don't behave, we'll leave.

I'm going to count to three.
It's amazing how she's grown.
If you don't behave, we'll leave.
I'm serious. We'll go home.

It's amazing how he's grown.
We come here on days like these.
I'm serious. You'll go home.
My God, she had wanted three.

We come here on days like these.
You stay with him. I'll take her.
And to think he wanted three.
It's hard to parent sober.

I'll go with him. You take her.
No, I'm not buying you that.
It's good to see you sober.
Has anyone seen a hat?

Mother's Day, 1961

When the Greyhound bus carrying
the freedom riders arrived,
a group of Klansmen were waiting,
some wearing their "Sunday best."
They shouted racial slurs, set fires,
and beat anyone they could reach
with bats, pipes, and chains.

In Birmingham, the police chief,
Bull Connor, explained why
the riders hadn't been protected
when everyone knew they were
coming. "It was Mother's Day,"
he said, "A lot of policemen were
at home with their mothers."

Lot's Wife

They appear on your computer or phone,
old photographs of your children
as toddlers, as first graders missing teeth,
water-skiing, sledding, cooking,
dressed for dances, games, graduations.
You see cars that you used to own
and colors the house used to be.
There is Lucy, that crazy black Lab,
and the gold fish, and, oh, the rabbit,
that's right, the rabbit that the kids
got to bring home from school
on the weekends. What grade was that?
The images appear, one after another,
jumping back and forth across years.
There you are putting together the crib
and the new bicycles and off they go,
driving away, now they are babies again,
and you wait for the next photo and the next,
unable to move, slowly turning to salt.

Navigating a National Cemetery on Memorial Day

Once they find the tombstone,
she complains about its location.
On the edge of a parking lot.
No view. No trees. No benches.
They say they doubt it's a slight.
Unless you're somebody, a hero,
an officer, you probably end up
wherever there's space. She says
it's typical of him and a lifetime
of getting bad tables and poor service
which meant she had a lifetime
of bad tables and poor service.
Now she's going to end up here?
Her name etched on the other side,
facing a brick wall and dumpsters?
They know these complaints are
a kind of grief. She says I know
once I'm here you won't even visit.
They say yes they will. Of course
they will. Just look at all this parking.

Memory Machines, or Cutting the Grass on Memorial Day Weekend

After wrestling the lawn mower out of the shed,
I discover it needs repairing, so I have to dig out
some tools from the cluttered storage area as well.
I negotiate the cramped space with care, no longer
having the strength or agility to just muscle things
around or slither smoothly through the bramble
of bikes, shelving, patio chairs, cords, tomato cages.
In the drive, I flip the mower over and consider it.
Such a turtled machine would have been a beacon
for the old men I grew up with; they would have
gathered, made suggestions, told stories. One priority
would have been to fix it, such jobs usually taking
exactly a six-pack of time. A second would have been
to comment on the shit design egghead engineers
had mistakenly insisted upon.

                             But I am alone.
If I need advice, I'll Google it, which is a wonder,
but Google can't tell me some things I want to know
like how old those old men were. I must be older
than them now although that seems impossible.
They were old. I'm not. Not like that. Although I know
to people passing by, I must look exactly like that:
a stooped man with no fashion sense, puttering
with machinery, more concerned about a nice lawn
than the turbulent state of the world. They don't know
it's a task I have always hated but grown resigned to.
They don't know I'm not that old. Not yet. Not yet.

Each Memorial Day Weekend, I think of those old men,
how they would all gather outside, lawn chairs in a circle
like a watch face, listening to the Indy 500 on radios
and tinkering on outboard engines. Once, contemplating
a disassembled Mercury, Uncle Freddy told me
to open the carburetor's butterfly. When I admitted

I didn't know where it was, he shook his head, saying,
*I always thought I would have a son and teach him how
to unstick a carburetor butterfly valve.* I didn't take it
as a criticism of my dad's parenting, but maybe it was.
Uncle Freddy had no kids, and was no relation, nor
was Aunt Lois, but they had the one happy marriage
in the neighborhood, holding hands on the swing or
idling around in a robin blue Hydrodyne speedboat
Uncle Freddy always had an unlit cigar in his mouth,
never taking it out even when he made his annual ski trip
around the lake on Fourth of July. He never smoked them;
he would chew and they would very slowly disappear.
A stub meant it was close to dinnertime. Finally Aunt Lois
convinced him to quit, and he switched to eating popcorn,
buckets and buckets full, until his death of colon cancer.

Once, we went into Uncle Freddy's house and found
he collected clocks. He had dozens, maybe hundreds,
stacked and piled everywhere, on shelves, under beds,
in closets. He fixed, refurbished, and researched them,
spending hours on these intricate machines. We asked
why he had so many, and he said only "I like clocks."
I wonder what it must have been like to be around
that ticking, all that time all the time, and if the clocks
had a connection to the childlessness and what Aunt Lois
thought of them and where they went after he died,
but there is no one to ask, not even Google. Time scatters.

There's not much light left in the day, so I work fast and
beerlessly, alone. The mower is electric, no carburetor,
and it does its job well enough, but I grouse as if in tribute
to those old men, *What a poorly designed piece of shit.*
This amuses me until I stumble on an extension cord, and
wonder what machine it is that I'm really talking about.

Cycling

Each year the city schedules Bulky Item Day,
and people drag old furniture and clutter
from attics, basements, and garages to the curb.
The week before, unfamiliar cars and trucks
begin to circle the blocks, picking and collecting.
Once I wheeled out a rusted bike, walked up
the drive, and turned around to find it gone.

For me, there is an excitement to the day,
a sense of possible treasures on every street,
a sense of relief at having so much weight
taken away, and it's fascinating to get glimpses
of who people were or who they wanted to be
—the exercise equipment and rowing machines,
the bunk beds for children long grown,
the four-stool pleather bar (no surprise since
their recycling bin had gone from being full
of whiskey bottles to Diet Coke cans).

One year I helped my daughter drag home
a broken wicker love seat. She patched it
with pink duct tape. When she left for college,
we put it back on the street, and it disappeared.

Like all holidays, this unofficial one celebrates
renewals, readjustments and recommitments,
and, it shows there are people who believe
they can make use of the obsolete broken parts
of a life. Sometimes I wonder if we should
designate a day to open our houses and
let people in. How would we see each other
afterwards? Would we be more understanding?
More generous? If they took something away,
would we better appreciate what remained?
Would we feel anxious or angry, or would we
feel lightened and follow them to the curb,
helping to load their selections, saying,
Thank you. Thank you so much. Thank you.

Spin

A neighbor puts an old washer at the curb
with the handwritten note, "This one limps along."
I think, "That could be on my year-end evaluations,"
and I remember the years of report cards that said,
"Joe needs to apply himself," or some version of
"I'm puzzled not to get better work from him."
I think how useful it would be to have such notes
on name tags for meetings. They could say, "This one
kind of listens," or "This one came for the donuts
but still is open to learning something new." If this
sounds negative or mocking, I think, "This one
limps along" is a tribute. It still works. It keeps going
despite its age and deterioration. And, after all,
isn't that the goal? That's what this one tells myself.

Advice Regarding Advice

No one wants a commencement speech
to be any longer, and, years from now,

no one will remember what was said,
or even who spoke. They are waiting

to go out with families and to parties.
They are waiting to go finish packing.

They are waiting to hear a name spoken
into the air, an incantation, a release.

They are waiting for a body to cross
space and begin its outward rippling.

Democracy: Cake or Yeast

After each election, we go to the doughnut store
to get the free treat given to those with a sticker
that says "I Voted." It's the only day I feel good
being in lines out the door, and I'm encouraged
by the holiday atmosphere, the patient waiting,
the belief, if only for a moment, in the rewards
of democracy. And in my town, after graduation,
seniors get a free dozen doughnuts, and they drive
around to different stores in their caps and gowns
in a giddy quest to pile box upon box. Afterwards
they meet somewhere, like when they were young
and sorted candy together after trick or treating.
It's what I wish for them throughout their lives,
such moments of abundance and community.

It's why as cynical as I may get sometimes
about National This or That Day, the ones
celebrating hamsters or chili dogs or snickerdoodles,
we always recognize National Doughnut Day
in our house. Make all the jokes you want;
dismiss it as crass consumerism, empty calories,
sugared decadence, but there is something
in these offerings, these circles squared in boxes,
that is important. It's food we eat bare-handed,
the weapons of knives and forks laid aside,
so it's altogether fitting and proper we come here
after casting our ballot. Because, while we can
hate a person abstractedly, it's different to be
confronted with the reality of a parent and child
happily eating a glazed doughnut or cinnamon twist
"I Voted" on whatever hat they may be wearing.

Loving Day

In the bedroom, they don't think about the color of their skin.
They think about how the other one has again kicked off the sheets.
They think about what that sound from the furnace might mean.
And in the kitchen, they don't think about the color of their skin.
They think about whether they should make another pot of coffee.
They think about if they'll need to stop by the grocery after work.
They think about how they never have the right Tupperware lids.
And in the garage, they don't think about the color of their skin.
They think about whether there is a better place to store the dog food.
They think about whose turn it is to mow the lawn this weekend.
They think about whether the car has enough gas for the commute.
But, sometimes, turning to one another, they do think about their skin.
They check one another for moles and changes. They apply lotion.
They trace each other's scars and lightly cover them with their hands.

Cleats

After practice, my son kicks off his cleats
and leaves them under the front seat.
He treats the van like a storage locker,
draping his uniform and sweats around.
The daughter complains each morning
as I take them to school. The cleats smell.
They're in her way. It's not fair. I agree
with all of these points, and yet I don't
tell the son to move them. For one,
it's yet another argument I'm too tired
to have. There are already so many things
I'm prodding him about: homework,
showers, closing doors, drinking water . . .
and, to be honest, I kind of like them there,
this mark of the boy, these muddy talismans.
He used to hold my hand as he fell asleep,
and once he pulled his fingers away,
picked his nose, then slid them back in my palm.
Yes, this is love, I thought then, holding snot
unflinchingly. Soon enough I'll be able
to keep the van and the house and my life
clean, uncluttered; for now, I let him
leave his cleats there, in everyone's way,
telling myself it's a type of civics lesson
about living together, telling my daughter,
"I know, I know, it's annoying. Kind of like
when someone keeps pre-setting the stereo
buttons to all their favorite stations." "No,
she says, "Oh, no. That is totally different."

What Apple Pie Tastes Like

On the Fourth of July,
I may be in Accident, Maryland,
with its small-town parade
of trailer floats promoting
local landscaping or dentistry
and where afterwards
the firefighters' auxiliary sells
hot dogs, hamburgers, chicken,
sugar cookies, chocolate cake
to raise money for equipment,

or I may be on the Chicago lakefront
where families arrive at dawn
to set up grills and tents,
hammocks and slacklines,
to play soccer, volleyball, badminton,
hackysack, cornhole, petanque,
chess, cards, dominoes, mahjong,
to strum guitars and sing karaoke,
and as I walk the shore, I hear
Spanish, Korean, Russian, Arabic,
English, Mandarin, French,
and I can buy tacos, shaved ice,
barbecue, empanadas, fruit,
popcorn, pierogies, potstickers,

or I may be in the back country
swapping trailmix with friends and
mixing Sharkleberry Finn KoolAid
with alcohol after a day of hiking,

but wherever I am I think of
the California poet drinking
in a New Mexico bar, and
of Benjamin Franklin and John Adams
having to share a room and arguing
about keeping a window open,
and of Hermey saying to Rudolph
as they flee oppression and wander
in fogs as thick as pea soup
or peanut butter, "What do you say
we be independent together."

Fireworks

i.
As the sun went down, we would arrange
lawn chairs, pillows, blankets, coolers full
of Pokagon pop, Tab soda, and Falstaff beer.
We would put out potato chips, pretzels,
discounted bags of broken Archway cookies,

then we would position ourselves to watch
the fireworks as if the sky was a screen,
a community gathering in the gloaming
waiting and wanting to be awed, eager
to applaud things set afire and blown up.

ii.
I was eight and watching *Planet of the Apes*
on a small black and white TV in the kitchen.
I didn't know the ship was called Icarus, and
I wouldn't have known what that meant,
but in college, when I heard "Ozymandias"
with its line "Nothing beside remains,"
I knew exactly what that meant because
I had seen the Statue of Liberty half-buried
in sand, an image that had me screaming
at the screen, "It's the earth! They're on earth!"

Growing up, a friend watched *The Wizard of Oz*
each year on her family's black and white TV.
Then in college, she went to a film screening
at a theater and when Dorothy opened the door
to Oz, she gasped, "Oh My God! It's in color!"
Everyone around her laughed, but she said for her
"It was like fireworks going off in my head."

iii.
July 1986, six months after
the Challenger disaster,
it was impossible to watch
smoke plumes across the sky
and not think of falling
bodies and debris

and years after that,
in the days of shock and awe
a reporter admitted ambivalence
because he wanted to say
the tracers and flares were beautiful,
like fireworks,

just as two hundred years earlier
Robert E. Lee observed, "It is well
that war is so terrible, otherwise
we should grow too fond of it," and

early in the Civil War people rode
carriages out to the battlefronts
taking picnic hampers and parasols.

iv.
Now, on the fourth of July,
a holiday that commemorates
not a battle—a victory or loss—
not the "rockets' red glare,"
but pens signing parchment,
ink instead of gunpowder
blowing up governments,
the dangerous possibilities
of an imaginative act,
I think of Ronald McNair,
an African-American male,

raised in the American South
in a home without electricity
or running water, who became
a physicist and astronaut
and how he brought a saxophone
on the Challenger,

and I think of Whoopi Goldberg
turning on the TV as a 9-year-old,
seeing Lieutenant Uhura of *Star Trek,*
and running through the house
screaming, "Come quick, come quick.
There's a black lady on TV
and she ain't no maid," and

I think of how that black lady,
Nichelle Nichols, was persuaded
not to quit the sci-fi series
by Martin Luther King Jr,
who told her it was the only show
he let his kids stay up to watch,

and I think of the memorials
at the Kennedy Space Center
for the Challenger and Columbia
that contain personal items of the crews,
photos, trophies, boy scout uniforms,
and how Michael P. Anderson's
has his Star Trek lunch box and thermos,

and I think of how fireworks
go off in our hands
and our heads, insisting
we look up, and how
America is a story
exploding across the sky.

Evening Song

Jack has brought a guitar, and, after the sessions,
he sits on the porch in the day's receding light
and plays Grateful Dead and John Prine songs.
Tim, a poet in the middle stages of dementia,
pushes his walker close and sits next to him.
They harmonize on "Ripple" and "U.S. Blues,"

and I remember how my college roommate
had hundreds of hours of bootlegs. Friday nights,
playing poker, we'd asked for something else, and
he would say "Yeah, okay, I'll put on Salt Lake '73."
When we would say, "Something besides the Dead!"
he would look at us puzzled. We lost touch years ago,

long before I actually began to listen to these songs,
before I learned words like "benign" and "malignant,"
before I worried about what it meant if I forgot a name.
As Jack and Tim harmonize with lifetimes of ghosts,
I'm stricken at what we lose—words, memories, friends—
and awed how some sing even as the darkness envelops.

The Shape of Cake

She says birthday cakes should be round,
like the years circling, like the wheel
of time and of life itself. She insists,
sheet cakes are bad luck, evil, wrong,
wrong, wrong, wrong, wrong, wrong.
They explain a sheet cake is easier to make,
particularly when baking with young kids
—there have been so many past disasters—
plus you can cut it into a lot more pieces.
She shakes her head, ease and options being
terrible criteria for something this important.
Years ago, someone had shown her a photo
of a drive-through wedding chapel at Vegas,
and she has heard you now can even confess
on-line. It has become a world of sheet cakes.
They listen patiently—this too being a part
of the ritual—then ask if she wants a piece.
"Of course I do," she says, "A big one please."

Call It Cake

She would make a cake for every celebration,
birthdays, holidays, graduations, but also
for regular visits and Saturday afternoons.
The making was so commonplace we never
bothered to learn the recipes. When she died
cakes disappeared from our lives (except
for grocery ones bought as an afterthought
or obligation). Eventually we recognized
what it had meant, her routine greeting
"I've made a cake." She had been saying,
Our time together is special. This day is special.
Let's celebrate. And so, finally, we learned
the lesson. Now, when we offer one another
a muffin, we call it cake. Wine? Call it cake.
This relationship? This life? Cake. Call it cake.

Party Planning in the Assisted Living Home

You ask what kind of cake they would like,
and they say, "I don't know. I'm not hungry."
You suggest cakes they've had in previous years
and they get annoyed. "Who wants an old cake?
Am I old and stale? Is that what you're saying?"
You know better than to respond. You suggest
chocolate, and they grimace. You ask, "Vanilla?"
and they recoil, "What would be the point of that?"
You say, "I just want to make something you like."
Their face changes. They lean in and whisper,
"I'll just have whatever Clint has." Their husband,
Clint, died years ago. You ask, "Does he like lemon?"
She nods, "Yes. With a lot of frosting. Too much."
You promise her there will be a lot, even too much.

Event Horizon

There comes a time you forget
a birthday or some other day
that used to have meaning—
an anniversary, a first date,
an adoption day, the finalization
of a divorce. The date slides by
frictionless, just a day of the week.

Or maybe it does snag slightly,
the numbers seeming vaguely familiar.
Didn't you use them as a passcode?
They must have been important.
You decide not to try to figure out why.
You walk the dog and take a photo
of a drawing chalked on the sidewalk.
You meet a friend for coffee.

Monday Morning, Illuminated

I carry my wife's workbag out to the car,
the way I have every weekday morning
for years. The sun is just under the horizon
so the houses and trees are silhouetted,
looking exactly like the design of a book
I used to read over and over to my son
called *When The Babies Crawled Away.*
In it, adults at a picnic eat and talk
and get distracted, the way adults do.
Only a young girl notices the babies
crawl away, and she goes after them.
Each time, my son would point to the girl
and say his older sister's name. He knew
she would follow and rescue him. He knew
she would protect him, and she did,
or tried to, for years. Now, I don't know
if they even speak to one another.
They have gone off in different directions,
and their occasional phone calls to us
only sketch rough outlines of their lives.
My wife comes out, grumbling at being late,
kisses me, then drives into the glimmering,
and although I know she'll return
as she does every evening, I also know
one day one of us will be here alone,
the other having "gone into the world of light"
as the poet says. I too have to get ready
for what's to come, which, today, is work,
but I keep looking at the houses and trees
and thinking about a book given away long ago,
how the details of our lives become obscured
until years, even decades, are suggested only
by phrases like "when the kids were young,"
and how all babies crawl away, eventually,

and no one can bring them back, and how
I should jot down some family stories
before they fade, and how there are old friends
I should contact, and how I just want to
keep standing here, watching this familiar story,
the arrival of the sun, the changing of the world.

Buffet

They think they would do better on their diet
if there just weren't so many fucking holidays.
Not just the major ones on that long decadent slide
after Halloween—Thanksgiving, December parties,
New Year's, Super Bowl, Valentine's Day—but
all the others. The birthdays, anniversaries,
vacations, celebrations, "Fridays," that pummel
them over and over. But they also know the problem
isn't really the holidays, but the people involved.
Their family and friends show love through food.
Alcohol and sugar. In quantity. When someone says,
"Do you want a piece of cake?" they are saying,
"I love you. Do you love me?" When her mother
has made a special trip to buy a special bottle,
refusing a drink would be like a slap in the face.
It's no wonder they're heavy, and they will stay so
until people stop caring for them, move away, or die.
At the doctor's office, as they get on the scale,
they tell the nurse with the clipboard, "This is not
my fault. I am loved. Not wisely, but too well."

Visitation

From my hotel room, I watch
the sun rise and illuminate a line
of cars circling a Starbucks
The light and line continually shifts
as I read about the poet Weldon Kees,
who in a conversation with a friend
asked, "What keeps you going?"
and the sadness of that question
flavors my coffee and morning.
He disappeared afterwards,
his car found with keys in the ignition,
and some say he either "killed himself
or went to Mexico," as if those, in the end,
are the only choices. Later, at the facility,
as I watch the line of boys with their scars
and burns, their dim eyes, their belief
nothing will help them, not the program,
not friendship, certainly not poetry,
I repeat silently, as if praying, "Please
choose Mexico. Wherever that may be.
Something there may keep you going."

What I Understand Now

As a child, I didn't understand much
of what the old women on the porch talked about.
When they would see someone walk by and say,
"I wouldn't kick him out of bed for eating crackers,"
I could tell it was a compliment by the tone,
but I didn't really know what it meant or why
they would laugh so much. It didn't occur to me
they were talking about sex. They were old, and
what would crackers have to do with sex anyway?

Sometimes we would ask where something was,
a coat, a toy, a container of leftovers in the fridge,
and our parents would say, "It's probably up
some fat lady's ass in Pittsburgh." I didn't know
what that meant either. In fact, even now I don't,
and I'm afraid to Google the phrase and start
an avalanche of unsavory emails and spam.

But, having become a parent, I do understand
at least the impulse to say something like it.
Since my children can't find their own fingers,
I'm constantly tempted to be sarcastic,
and I constantly succumb. I understand now
about frustration, repetition, resignation,
the ridiculousness involved in living
with others, even the surreal possibility
that maybe everything we've misplaced
is somehow ass-deep in Pittsburgh.

And, yes, I understand about the crackers,
what you put up with for someone attractive,
the crumbs, the crunch, the irritations.
I know now about the untidiness of desire,
the bill you pay for it, sometimes willingly,
and the way you mock it as you get older.

I think I'm even beginning to understand
the complex laughter of those old women
sitting on the porch and talking about sex,
how they understood the absurdity
of aging into these lives, these bodies,
those heavy old women who probably were
younger and thinner than I am now.

Guttering

He has been doing this for decades,
climbing the ladder to clean out
rotting leaves, twigs, whirligigs.
In retrospect, perhaps he should
have bought gutter guards long ago,
but they couldn't afford them at first,
then there were always other expenses,
schools, vacations, cars, medical bills,
and who knew they would live here
this long? It still seems day-to-day.

Once, when the kids were young,
he insisted that they and their friends
weren't responsible enough to clean
the gutters, and each one had demanded
the chance to climb and scoop muck.
A fine Tom Sawyer trick on his part.
In those years, he would find tennis balls,
frisbees, army men, and once sunglasses
from one of his daughter's break-ups.
Now it's just the autumn debris of trees.

For a while he suggested there should be
a National Gutter Day when we clean out
what's collected over the year and is now
clogging us, a day we get out trash bags,
put on gloves, and clean the channels.
The Day wouldn't necessarily involve
climbing rungs, but could be walking
with an old friend, having a coffee, or
dropping off boxes at the Goodwill,
or it might mean putting up new gutters
in places they haven't been, a relationship
with a parent, friend, lover or neighbor,
recognizing a need to separate and sluice

away what might damage the foundations.
Then he realized that day was New Year's
with its resolutions, and he did chores
like this on holiday weekends anyway—
Easter, Memorial Day, Labor Day—
and who would want to swap out, say,
Fourth of July for National Gutter Day?
Plus he had vague memories of an uncle,
a Navy vet, who would talk about the need
to get drunk and "get his pipes cleaned out,"
and he could see how National Gutter Day
could become "End Up in the Gutter Day,"
a bacchanalia, like St. Patrick's or Mardi Gras,
which is not what he meant, so he stopped
making that suggestion. Now he surveys
the neighboring yards and houses of friends
long gone, of children grown, and remembers
another joke, one about Jesus they loved to tell
in Catholic school with its punchline of Christ
saying to Peter, "I can see your house from here."
He feels he understands the joke more each year,
the dark humor in the face of mortality, the pull
of the banal even as a life gutters towards its end.
It occurs to him there could be a good variation
of the joke, something along the lines of "Peter,
I can see you need to clean your gutters," and
then he realizes this aligns him with Christ, and
he laughs at such arrogance and ridiculousness.
He still has enough self-awareness to know
it probably makes the neighbors nervous, seeing
an old man angled in the air, sporadically laughing
and appearing morose. He wonders how long
he can continue to do this, but they can't afford
to pay a neighbor kid, even if they knew one.
He still expects to hear her come out and yell

in that angry voice that shows worry and love,
"Jesus, get down!"(or "Jesus get down!") but
she stays inside now. In bed. Trying to cough
the muck in her lungs clear. When he's finished,
he'll make her tea and tell her how the people
in the McCaffrey place have painted the kitchen.

He thinks it's just as well they never bought
the guards. Some maintenance is good to do
on his own, to remember old jokes, to plunge
his hands into the year's decay, and to prepare,
as best as he can, for the storms that are to come.

Harvest Moon

After dinner, I walk the dog in the dark,
and as we climb a neighborhood hill,
the moon seems to push its way into the sky
and rises through the trees, becoming so large
and luminous I stop, unable to continue.

Unlike the horse in Frost's poem,
the dog is used to such paralysis from me.
She sniffs tree trunks and leaf piles,
biding her time, while I gape upwards.

Stunned.

Eventually, I take out my phone
—not to take a picture which would only reduce
this glowing globe to a dot, a disappointment
—but to message my daughter who is grown
and gone. I text "The Moon!" and she knows
this means, "Quick. Go outside!" She knows
this means, "The universe is beautiful, isn't it?"
She knows this means, "I miss you. I love you."

I feel I should do more. I should knock on doors
and tell people to come out. I'm not possessive.
There's enough moon to go around. I know
some of my neighbors and know they might
appreciate such witnessing, but I also recognize
they might be more impressed with my "sensitivity"
than the moon itself, which would be frustrating.
I deserve no credit. Minutes ago, I didn't know
it was a full moon tonight. How is that possible?
Why has this miracle again surprised me? Why
haven't I put on my calendar a recurring event
or To Do item: "Be Astounded!"

              I don't knock on doors.
Instead I kneel by my dog and text my child, who,
having gone outside, texts back, and we are happy
to be in contact, miles apart, the moon connecting,
the moon astonishing, our mundane lives spectacular.

Autumn

After we turn in grades, we go on a hike,
picking a trail we've never done before
even though we've lived here for decades.
We're careful because it's on hunting land.
We crunch the fallen leaves loudly, talk
loudly, say occasionally, "I'm not a deer!"
loudly. The sky is a crisp, painful, blue.
There are views through the bare trees
that wouldn't be seen in other seasons.
We talk about books and films. We talk
about the map and the trail signs. We talk
about our families and finances, a coffeeshop
that's opened downtown, a restaurant
that has recently closed. At some point,
they mention the most recent lab results,
the doctors' estimates. I share trail mix.
They offer slices of apple. We begin to walk
faster because the days are shorter now,
the path unfamiliar and quickly growing dark.

Braids

When my daughter was young, she loved to play hair-dresser.
I would sit on her ABC rug, and she would put a wig or towel
over my balding head, then brush and style for hours, chatting

about the difficulties of running a business and raising kids.
Now, years later, I pay her for haircuts, and as I sit on a stool,
she tells me about school and the choices her friends are making.

Often as she rotates around me, I imagine some future visit,
me in assisted living, her borrowing scissors from the staff.
They say hair continues to grow after death, and I hope it's true.

I hope my daughter will keep cutting my hair until she too is old,
that she will keep talking to me, seeing the man who loved her
enough to sit on a floor for hours patiently holding a stuffed bear,

the way I still see a girl with afro-puffs, adorned in Disney jewelry,
telling me not to be afraid, telling me she will make me beautiful.

What We Carry

A family of five, we trailered
a pop-up tent on highways
all around the country,
camping in state parks,
picnicking in rest areas.
It was how we could afford
to go anywhere. Each of us
had a beer case in which
we could put whatever
we needed or wanted.
T-shirts, toiletries, snacks.
I filled mine with comic books,
choosing to wear the same outfit
for an entire trip to make room
for Archie, Batman, Casper,
Richie Rich, the Fantastic Four,
Spider-Man, Tales from the Crypt,
Two Fisted War Stories, and
I would read for mile after mile
after mile after mile after mile.

Annoyed, my father would say,
Put those damn comic books down
and look out the window.
You may never be here again!
I would glance up to see
some mountain or forest or
tourist attraction, say "cool,"
then go back to reading.
Years later, I hear his voice
in mine as I tell my children
to get off their phones
and *Look at that! Look! Look!*

I understand my father now,
his desire for us to be present,
but I was traveling elsewhere
as we crossed Ohio or Nebraska.
Before I ever heard of multi-verses,
I knew what they were. They were
stacked in that beer box. They were
pages and panels. They were worlds
made by words and images. They were
stories we travelled with and in, ones
we needed more than clothes or food.

Seasons Greetings!

In his way, Clancy was being generous,
recognizing that Jews had holidays too,
and seeing one listed on the calendar
of the office, he had decided to feature it
on the restaurant's big marquee sign.

HAPPY YOM KIPPUR!
10% OFF EXTRA LARGE PIZZAS!

It was the one time we saw Benny angry.
He would ignore jokes about the Holocaust
or comments about being a Christ killer
with a thick skin we all respected,
but when he saw the sign, he came in,
dragged Clancy from the register, yelling
"My grandmother drives past here, asshole,"
and slammed him against the freezer door.

After we separated them and calmed Benny,
we tried to point out that Clancy had been
assuming a kind of equivalency in holidays:
Merry Christmas equals Happy Hannukah.
Happy Easter equals Happy Yom Kippur.
Benny explained it was the difference between
saying Happy Easter or Happy Good Friday,
and we recognized how that might be seen
as offensive. He explained it was a sacred day
of fasting, of atonement, of confession,
and we agreed Happy Atonement!
Happy Fasting! Happy Confession!
Happy Please Put Me in the Book of Life
for Another Year! didn't sound like something
Pepsico Inc. would want on the marquee.

Clancy apologized, went out and changed
the top half of the sign's message to:

TRY OUR CHEESY GARLIC BREAD!

Then later, at shift's end, he got high with Tracy,
the assistant manager, and they talked for a while
about Jews, looked through the policies manual,
and filled out a report, sending Benny's name
to corporate and recommending termination.

Skeletons in the Waffle House

If you get there and the Waffle House is closed? That's really bad. . .
—Craig Fugate, Former Head of the Federal Emergency
Management Agency

When the trick or treating is over,
we end up here, as we usually do
after a work shift, a dance, a date.

It's comforting to know exactly
what we're going to get, no matter
who we are at the moment, a skeleton,
a ghost, a jilted lover, a single parent.

The staff doesn't care. They've seen it all
year after year. The faces and bodies
and costumes change; the coffee doesn't.

So, when we go towards the light, perhaps
we shouldn't be surprised if we discover
it's a Waffle House sign, the first place
to open after an emergency or disaster.

Growth

Smoking stolen cigarettes behind the garage,
talking about cars, jobs, girls, all vaguely
since we knew little about any of them,
occasionally someone would mention someone
they knew who'd had a tumor removed.
They would list details like size—
big as a grapefruit—weight—five pounds—
or bizarre characteristics like it had hair
and teeth. And always, the person had no idea.
They had gone to the doctor for something else,
because they were tired, feeling "poorly,"
thought they were pregnant. These stories
were more terrifying than Halloween films
or Scary Woods. Even young and ignorant
we understood how horror is carried within,
often unknowingly. Later we would appreciate
the beauty of the words "benign" and "remission."
Later we would understand why some insisted
on fiercely celebrating each holiday they could.

Souling

There was not much that was ahead of him,
And there was nothing in the town below—
Where strangers would have shut the many doors
That many friends had opened long ago.
                    —E.A. Robinson, *Mr. Flood's Party*

i.

Then came the year the youngest was too old
to go trick or treating. They wanted to go
to a friend's party instead. And I felt the barb
of time's arrow tug at me. That night,
not yet wanting to be alone in the house,
I wandered the streets along the familiar route,
one my children and their friends had mapped
over years of Octobers. They knew the houses
that encouraged you to take handfuls from the bag
and the ones that simply put out a bowl with a note
so you had to get there before someone emptied it,
the house where a huge spider descended and
the one where the guy jumped out with a chain saw.

Alone, I placed a different map on top of theirs.
On that corner, my oldest, at six, had gone ahead
into the street, and when I stopped her, she spun
in defiance, yelling "You're not the boss of me."

In that tree, we hung the mask of a costume
they had begged for and quickly began shedding.

That house and that one had friends who would
pour wine or whiskey into the parents' To Go cups.

At that intersection, one year the older kids annoyed
at the slowness of the siblings had asked to run ahead
and within seconds had disappeared into the night.

Surrounded by ghosts on the sidewalks, I realized
walking without a child probably made me scary
and there were no doors that would open with drinks
for me anymore. I returned to my dark dwelling.

ii.
The youngest came home late, dissatisfied.
The party hadn't been much fun,
so they had gone trick-or-treating after all,
but that too had been disappointing.
He didn't know the neighborhood,
no one had wanted to run from house to house,
and afterwards they didn't lie on the floor
to sort and swap what they had gathered.
Not that they had much. It turned out
teenagers, making half-assed gestures
at costumes with a hat or orange shirt,
don't get showered with treats, not like
six-year-old monsters, witches, and pirates.
So, unlike other years when he would be
too candy-crazed to sit still, he was thoughtful,
processing the discovery he was no longer young
and cute, no longer fussed over. The holiday
no longer seemed his; he had wanted so badly
to be older, not realizing what he would lose.

iii.
Writing this now I remember how much
I complained each fall, how I often said
I hated Halloween because a girl
I thought I loved broke up with me
twice—both times on October 31—
(once dressed as a nurse, once as a crayon),
how the holiday was weird, the way
it romanticized threats and violence,
sexualized young girls and professions,
how it had been hijacked by adults
gratifying their Peter Pan impulses.

And I remember how I used to mock
the soul song "You Don't Miss Your Water"
with its explanation "till your well runs dry."
Couldn't you see it running dry?
I would sneer. Couldn't you anticipate
missing it? But I was wrong, as I've been
about so many things. I didn't recognize
how even as I was ranting, and considering
Halloween an obligation, another set
of artificial ritualized parental duties,
there is something wonderful about
walking in the dark with those you love,
young and playful and hopeful, pretending
to be other people, each house a party,
your bounty increasing door by door.

iv.
Here you go, Daddy, the youngest said,
handing me a bite-size Almond Joy
I know these are your favorite.

Ghosts

When you're young,
you don't realize how many
ghosts are at the table
during the holidays,
helping in the kitchen,
suggesting recipes,
making music selections,
or that they've been invited.

Later, you'll hear them coming,
hanging their coats in the hall,
laughing and making jokes,
arguing about something
that happened a lifetime ago,
the lullaby of family.

When finally you are in charge
and can put decorations
exactly as you want,
you still do things
as they've been done before.
The ghosts nod, satisfied,
agree to come back next year.

Veterans Day

Every year she buys him socks as a gift.
Warm ones. Thick ones. Thermals. Woolens.
He doesn't need them. He has drawers full,
but he always seems genuinely grateful,
much to the bewilderment of the children.

For two years in that war, he felt he never could
get his feet dry and warm and he was sure that
he was going to die. He would write her the first,
not the second, but she knew, just as she knows
the shape of love isn't a heart, but a foot.

Winter Night, Music Lesson

However the fight started—dirty dishes in the sink,
something broken, general truculence—at some point,
my father decided I needed to practice my clarinet more,
and that I do so right then. "This begins now,"
he had yelled, citing the costs, the band classes,
the holiday concert he surprisingly knew about,
the fact he had never heard me play at home.
He insisted I get out the case and sheet music, and
when I did, we discovered I didn't have any reeds.
This enraged him. "You've been pretending at school!"
He began calling other families to see who had a child
who played an instrument and might have a reed.
Finally he left—I thought to go back to the bar—and
I fell asleep. Hours later, he returned, clutching,
a box of Vandoren B flats like a pack of cigarettes.
God knows where he had gotten them so late,
perhaps he had stumbled from house to house
until he found someone with a kid in band.
He shook me awake, and insisted I play. I did.
A few notes from "Flight of the Bumblebee."
That's all I knew, or ever would. It satisfied him,
and we both went to bed. I think often of this moment.
It has a lesson in it. For someone. About something.

Giblets

My father stuck his hand into the turkey
and pulled out a plastic bag like a magic trick.
Shocked, we asked, "What are those?"
"Giblets," he said, "Your grandma loved them."
The explanation left us no better informed.
"Heart, liver, gizzard, neck." He recited
the parts in a horrifying off-hand manner.
What were they doing stuffed up there?
"Giblets," we said, tasting the odd word.
"What did she do with them?" we asked.
"Made them into gravy or fried them.
She never wasted anything. She reused
tin foil again and again. She saved string.
String! I didn't know what I wanted to be
when I grew up, but I knew one thing.
I didn't want to be poor." He held the bag
in his hand as if weighing it. We watched
to see what he would do, uneasy; sometimes
he made us try new things. There was
the scrapple incident. And the liver mush.
We were relieved when he pitched the bag
in the trash, saying with disgust, "giblets,"
and yet, that made us uneasy as well.

How to Break Your Hand

When your parents visit for the holidays,
like they've done so many times,
have cleared the counters of the rubble
of daily living, have cleaned the house,
have swept the sidewalks and steps,
but have one of them suddenly trip on—
who knows—a root? a rock? a twig?—
seemingly nothing, and have them fall
and badly scrape their knee, elbow, face.
Help lift them and get them to a chair.
Get band aids from the kids' bathroom.
Have them choose between Sponge Bob
and Spider-Man. Later that night,
once they're in bed, remember how,
when you bought the house years ago,
they helped with the renovations,
easily carrying 2x4s from the van
and painting on the step ladders.
Think about the fall and what's coming.
Slam your hand against the kitchen tiles.

The Company We Keep

We had spent this holiday with them for years,
always bringing a bottle of wine and a dessert
to put among the antique table settings, and
each time they would serve generous helpings
of irritation and outrage, and we would try
to put as little as possible on our plates.
They would insist we take home leftovers,
they would promise to send recipes,
they would say how wonderful it had been.
Finally, one year, we decided not to go.
Instead we ordered takeout and then
went for a walk through the neighborhood.
We marveled at how loud the birds were.
We asked, "Have they always been here?"

Traditions

Claire scoffs at the dining room table's centerpiece,
a decoration of a pilgrim and turkey hugging,
and insists that it's kitsch at best, and, at worst,
a smiley face put on genocide. Sherry isn't sure
what either of these mean, but knows neither
is a compliment. She gives her daughter a hug
and says, "I just have always thought it's funny.
When you have your own house, you can put
out whatever you want." Claire says, "I won't
celebrate dumb holidays like this." Her mother
knows better than to pursue this conversation
and says, "I'm just glad that you come home."

Jack announces he has become a vegetarian
because his girlfriend is, and this way they can
share food, but he doesn't like mashed potatoes,
cranberries, or pumpkin pie, so he's going to order
DoorDash in a bit if anyone wants to go in with him.
Bill says if that's the reason then Jack might as well
eat turkey today since he's alone and hasn't paid
for any of it, and Jack says Bill doesn't understand.
Bill says, "I understand the longer you're in school
the dumber you get," and then he goes out back.
He used to watch football throughout the day,
but his team has sucked for years, and he's decided
a concern with head injuries has spoiled the game,
so he drinks in the garage and listens to talk radio.

Molly used to sit at the table before the meal,
stacking coupons in piles between place settings
and planning out a Black Friday route, but now
she does all her shopping on her phone, saying
periodically to Sherry, "Let me know if you need
any help. Is there enough gravy this year? I think
maybe sometimes we haven't had enough gravy."

When the dinner is ready, they gather at the table, sitting at the places they each have sat at for years. In lieu of a prayer, Sherry says, "Dorothy's right. There's no place like home." Claire snorts loudly, "Well that's an ambiguous statement, isn't it?" Molly says, "I've never understood why she leaves the wonderful world of Oz where she's a princess to go back to ugly depressed Kansas." Bill shrugs, "She got her bell rung. No concussion protocols," and Jack decides to have some potatoes after all.

In My Kitchen, Depressed, I Think of Richard Feynman Dancing

While in college, he agreed to go to a hotel
with two women because he was curious
about what would happen. He discovered
they wanted to go to a dance for people
who, like them, were deaf and dumb.

He spent the evening there and later said
how wonderful it was, the not knowing
and then learning, the moving together,
the music heard in different ways,
the communication in different ways.

After he helped build the atomic bomb
in Los Alamos while his wife was dying
in a nearby sanatorium, he lost all desire
to work on anything for a couple years.
After all, what was the point?

Then, he began to play with cafeteria plates
making observations about their spinning,
his curiosity reemerging like water from
an irrepressible well. When Hans Bethe said,
"Feynman, that's pretty interesting,

but what's the importance of it?
Why are you doing it?" He replied,
"There's no importance whatsoever.
I'm just doing it for the fun of it."
Now Feynman and Bethe are dead, and

those he danced with in college are dead,
yet I continue to be moved by moments
from their lives. I spin in the kitchen and
sign the word for milk and sign the word
for life and sign the word for Thank you.

Thanksgiving

There is no need for turkey,
stuffing, cranberries, pies.
There is nothing that needs
to be served at the table.
There is no need for leftovers.
There is no need for a table.

There is no need to endure
crowded airports and highways.
Love shouldn't be compelled
by the calendar and clock.

There is no need to take notice
of any of the events, the parades,
games, sales, that seem, at best,
cultural non-sequiturs, at worst,
obscenities for a holiday rooted
in trauma, famine, war, suffering.

What is needed?
                    Nothing
but a willingness to surrender
expectations and give thanks

for what you can, when you can,
whether it's on the fourth Thursday
in November, the second Monday
in October, or a random weekend.

Give thanks without any trappings
and trimmings. Whisper thanks
as you wait in line or get dressed.
Then do it again. Give thanks
for what food you have. Give thanks
for friends and family, no matter

when you last saw them. Give thanks
for strangers who acknowledge you
and for those who leave you alone.
Give thanks for the light and the dark.
Give thanks that you are able to give
thanks. Give thanks until you are full.

Black Friday

i.
Jack trades a cow
for a few beans,
and part of us
agrees with his mother
even when we know
what will happen—
He's an idiot.
He was taken—
and part of us hopes
to make a sweet deal
like that someday.

ii.
We roam store aisles
wanting to believe
we can buy something
to show we care.
We can turn coins
into sweaters
into love
and, yes, there may be
tragic consequences
in faraway lands
where the goods come from
but, like Jack,
not for us.

iii.
We know magic
involves deception,
a sleight-of-hand,
the French drop,
misdirection,
and yet we never ask
the name of the vendor

who sold the beans.
We never ask
why they would
make such a trade.
We never ask where
they slipped off to
while we watched Jack.

Horses

I know people who know horses.
They ride them and own them
and talk about their different points.
They look at a horse in a field or paddock
and assess it, speaking of its attributes.
In the Westerns I read growing up,
there were always characters who knew
"horse flesh." I don't. I know nothing.
All horses are beautiful to me.

Home Alone

Having inched up the ladder's rungs,
holding the looped decorations like rope,
you remember your brother's comment,
No one should get on a roof after fifty,
and the fact you promised your partner
you wouldn't clean out the gutters
when no one was home. Technically
this is different, and you are doing it
for her since she loves Christmas lights.
But, even though you're not on the roof,
just a ladder, high (very high) in the air,
it's not the climbing, but the reaching
to twist the cord around a nail or eyelet,
it's the leaning, that puts you at risk,
because, to be honest, in years past,
it hasn't felt like leaning, just a motion
that needed to be done. You balanced
without thinking about balancing; now,
you're aware of it, and being aware
makes it awkward and dangerous. Is this
the least realistic part of the Santa myth?
An old guy so sure-footed on shingles?
You want to believe, not in him, but
in yourself, that you can move around,
irrespective of gravity, and yet you know
one misstep, one inch cantilevered too far,
will forever change the holiday season.
You realize now, although the movies
and cards never show it, riding shotgun
with the fat man in red is the gaunt one
with the scythe. You don't look down
to see their bony fingers on the rungs.

Defender of the Faith

She tells her mother there's been talk
on the playground about Santa Claus
not being real. "Some kids," she shrugs,
the way one might say "nut jobs" or
"punks" or "heretics." At the same time,
they're insisting God exists. It's puzzling.
Her mother asks, "What do you think?"
which takes the daughter aback. Long ago
she recognized a response like that
usually means something is going unsaid.

The next afternoon when her mother asks,
"How was school?" she says, "Fine" then
begins pulling papers out of her backpack
as if it is a lawyer's briefcase. She had been
in the attic, rummaging its holiday boxes,
and in the cabinet with its folders of her work.
She has gathered evidence. "See," she says,
"Santa has written to me. Letters. Cards.
Plus there are photos. And the government
tracks his sled each year." Case closed.
Her mother asks how people responded;
she says, "Bobby insisted only babies believe
in Santa. I said, 'Oh yeah, you got a letter
from Jesus? Let's see it.' That shut him up."

secret

they carry a dreidel in a pocket and spin it
to make decisions but don't tell anyone sometimes
they spin it in their mind nothing all half add one
they know what it means and what it is suggesting

like any good reader of tarot or divination sticks
they know they are supposed to admire the heroes
the ones who wear the capes and they know
the history of the two jews in 1930s cleveland

creating the assimilation savior story of superman
but there are many ways to work through
the trauma of existence like scarred harry dent
with a scarred coin in his pocket growing up

they have heard the stories of how the dreidel
made it seem as if people were just playing
a game when they were actually reading
the forbidden torah but they weren't offended

when someone pointed out there is no dreidel
mentioned in old texts and it probably comes
from christian traditions but then christ was born
in the spring and the declaration of independence

was voted on july second and who knows
the name of bill finger you spin from youth
to adulthood choosing what stories to follow
what to tell in part or full and what to keep

secret

Rituals

The first Christmas after the divorce,
Mr. Nelson put up a small white tree
in the bay window and then left it there.
We thought that was crazy, in a fun way,
although we never rang his doorbell
at Halloween or offered to shovel his drive
when we were trying to make some money.
Mom would sigh if anyone mentioned it,
saying "those poor children." Dad, however,
grew increasingly annoyed, even angered,
and each holiday as he put up decorations,
he would mutter about doing things right
not like Chuck Nelson who didn't give
a good goddamn anymore, who was making
a mockery of everything. This too became
a holiday ritual, one that surprised me
because my father hated the obligations
that came with owning a house. Later,
when I had a place of my own, each time
I searched around the attic for the boxes
we seemed to have just put away, I thought
of Mr. Nelson. It made a certain sense.
Why take down a tree only to put it up again?
Plenty of people don't make their beds. And,
later still, at the funeral, I talked to Jeff Nelson,
one of "those poor children," the only one,
who came, and he explained how his mother
always had complained about the holidays.
The cooking and decorating and shopping
exhausted her, and she felt no one appreciated
her efforts to be a "good mother." The divorce,
Jeff said, had liberated them all. Afterwards,
each made their own haphazard way through
the year, ignoring most holidays, buying a cake
for a birthday, but only if they felt like it. I asked

what would happen to the white tree by the casket.
He shrugged. "Dumpster. That was a holiday
that Dad needed," and I felt an odd stab of regret,
recognizing maybe we should have rung the door
to trick-or-treat. Maybe on snow days we should
have trudged up and offered to clear a path. Maybe
it had been us who hadn't given a good goddamn.

Home and the Holidays

Pumpkin spice, peppermint, cinnamon, pine,
these are the mass-market tastes and scents
of the holidays, evoking a generic nostalgia
akin to the music of school band concerts.
Not offensive, but not particularly intense.
For a shiv-sharp memory, it needs to be personal.
For me, it's the Velveeta my mother used
in her "holiday dish," green beans with cheese
that we ate on Thanksgiving and Christmas.
For you? I don't know. You might not either
until you're in someone's kitchen and see a label
on a condensed milk can or a pack of Kool menthols
and suddenly you're nine again and vaguely aware
there are things happening you don't understand,
like the shouting and crying in the driveway
or why your parents keep those old photos
of strangers in their bedroom dresser drawers.

Those of Us with Bushy White Beards

We've all been called Santa at some point,
especially if we've gained a little weight
as we've aged. Maybe a kid has even reached
for the whiskers. We get it, they look so soft.
Some of us ignore the glances and comments
from the nearby tables. Some of us ask
for discounts for our coffee with a low chuckle.
Some of us begin to work a little more red
into our wardrobe. We feel, if not a responsibility,
at least an awareness, and we nod to each other
the way bikers tip their fingers in passing.
We are Wearers of the Beard. The Claus chapter.
There are others. The Hemingways. The Lincolns.
The Civil War Generals. The Lebowskis. The Vikings.
Once in a lobby, I met a young brown-bearded man.
Jesus! I exclaimed and received a familiar rueful smile.
We stopped, faced off, and gestured to one another:

After you.

No, no, after you.

No, I insist.

as bystanders watched, delighted and a little uneasy.

Flashing

One year, you had heard them, sleigh bells on the roof,
and your excitement had made it impossible to sleep.
Later, when the "truth about Santa" began to circulate
on the playground, your faith stayed firm long after
others had denied him. After all, you had heard the bells.
But, eventually, you became embarrassed for how
stupid you had been and for how long you had believed,
and the memory became bitter. Pathetic, such delusion.
It was a cautionary story, and sometimes you'd tell it
in a performance of self-mockery turning your naivete
and embarrassment into an amusing party anecdote.
Then one December, visiting your father in the home,
the staff had decorated a tree and perched a Santa hat
on his head. When you snatched it off, he laughed and,
surprisingly lucid, he began to reminisce about how good
Christmases had been, how hard they had always tried
to make them special for the kids. Once, they had even
borrowed sleigh bells and shook them in the attic.
He didn't notice you stiffen and pull away. You had to
leave the room, and, when you returned, once again
he no longer knew who you were, but he recognized
what you held in your hand. "I like your hat," he said.

Here We Go A-Caroling (Again and Again and Again and Again)

How is it we hear these songs
hundreds of times, year after year,
and still don't know the lyrics?

At the opening notes,
we may start off strong,
even getting through the first verse
to belt the chorus,
but then
we begin to mumble
then hum
then fall silent and simply sway
until the chorus again.

Even if we know the words,
we may not know their meaning.
"Repeat the sounding joy"?
"Troll the ancient Yule-tide carol"?
"God rest ye merry gentlemen"?

Who is "Good King Wenceslas"?
And it seems statistically unlikely
"we all like our figgy pudding."

We're born into songs and stories,
whose meanings have been as upsot
as the sleigh in "Jingle Bells,"
and yet we are comforted
by these repetitions and their mysteries.

We gather and we sing,
loudly if sporadically,
our lives a muddle of sounding joys.

The Elf's Holiday

Among the misconceptions and stereotypes,
the most annoying one is the idea we love
to work from one Christmas to the next,
cheerfully, with no breaks, no vacations,
as if the only holiday is death, as if that final
goodbye should be called The Elf's Holiday.
How poetic that would be to some. I'm sure
there would be sentimental pictures in homes
of the final passing of the elf, the noble worker,
now gone to their reward. But that's just crap.
Sentimental Tiny Tim Hallmark movie bullshit.
We take vacations, ones we not only deserve, but,
to Santa's disgust, are written into our contracts,
and it's "Elves Gone Wild" or "What Happens
on Elf Holiday Stays on Elf Holiday." There is
a key difference though. We don't go to Vegas
or on Carnival cruises. Among the drunks there
we wouldn't stick out—which would be good—
but it also would seem too close to work. We want
the opposite. No forced fake "fun" celebrations.
We go to Indiana. Iowa. Flyover states. We drink
in bars with neon signs for cheap beer. We stay
in the middle of a week at Motel 6s on the edge
of industrial towns. We have a brief time to drink
and fuck—on our own terms—and we do. And
I wonder if right now some of you are offended,
more by the idea of elves fucking, or just the word,
"fucking," than by the idea of us having to work
most of our lives to make the cheap crappy gifts
you put in drawers, often unused, often unworn.
What do you need to ignore about how your luxuries
are made? What sentimental myths and lies do you
need to tell yourselves? That we're not like you?
That we don't like to drink or screw? Oh, but we do,
and, by the way, The Sugar Plum Fairy does too.

Nostalgia

More years than not
the tree got knocked down

because of dogs,
or parties, or fights,

but mostly because
the holiday season
was a drinking season,

and each time the tree
would be levered back up,
broken ornaments swept up,
decorations cleaned up,
water mopped up,

so the next night
the tree seemed as bright,

and maybe outside
no one could tell
anything had happened,

and maybe for some
that would have been reassuring,
things can be set aright,

but once you know
how it can come down,
whether by accident or anger,
it never seems aright again.

Accumulation

When the couple bought the ornament
for one of their first Christmases together,
it was nothing special, just part of a box
of a dozen cheap red and gold bulbs
that they could afford at Woolworths.
Now, it's the only one remaining of the set,
having withstood pets, toddlers, teenagers,
parties, grievings, packings and unpackings,
and its survival has made it precious enough
to store in tissue and handle like a reliquary.

In the future, after the couple dies,
at some point, the children or grandchildren
will have to decide who gets it and all
the other decorations. They might fight
over it, or perhaps they will pass it around,
or it will be put in a pile with clothing,
books, dishes, the bric-a-brac that eddies
into a life and gets sluiced to a Goodwill.
One day it probably will be shattered
in a moment of clumsiness or conflict,

but, for now, each December the aged bulb
is unwrapped, held aloft for contemplation,
then placed in the boughs among the others,
ones made as elementary school projects,
ones given by family, friends, colleagues.
Ornament by ornament, a tree becomes
an accumulation of memories, transforming
trinkets into a comfort of color, a testament
in a dark time to what has been saved and
what, for another year, remains unbroken.

Boxes

There is a list I'm keeping called
"What I Would Have Done Differently"
because I'm expecting that question
on Judgement Day, and I'm preparing,
like for any interview or evaluation.

Each year the list gets longer.
That's the annoying part of living.
You think you'll get better at it.
But you don't. Even if you think
you do, you're wrong. I know

there are things they will be expecting,
the usual sins and obligatory regrets,
and maybe these are what they want
to hear, pro-forma boxes to check,
but first on my list? Getting better

storage bins for the decorations.
Each year I just shoved the lights
haphazardly back into the attic,
acting as if it was a one-shot deal,
and I wouldn't need them again,

but the holidays kept coming around,
and sturdy boxes would have been
worth the investment. If this answer
seems to disappoint, if they find it
shallow, I'll explain that's exactly

what I thought and why I didn't act.
When I was young, I told my mother
taking out the garbage was trivial
in the grand scheme of things. I was
thinking big thoughts, and so trash

piled up, week after week, chores
were haphazardly done, and our lives
together were diminished. I'll try
to explain my misunderstandings
about time, how I didn't appreciate

the repetition and speed and beautiful
banality of it all, and, yes, how I believe
better boxes would have helped. Or
maybe I'll skip to the latest item I've put
on the list. Take better care of my teeth.

Outing, New Year's Eve

We take the kids to a bar
in the early afternoon
before the lights dim
and serious drinking starts.

There's the anticipation
of a party to come,
the feeling when a snow day
has been forecasted.

The bartender opens a carton
of plastic top hats and tiaras
to give them the first ones.
We have Cokes. We toast.

On the way home, the kids
roll their windows down,
blow horns and kazoos,
shout "Happy New Year!"

We circle the block
searching for people
to joyously accost
with good wishes

revelling in this
unplanned moment,
the giddiness of being
together making noise.

The Holiday Cycle

He complains about seeing Halloween displays
when school hasn't even started yet. She listens
to the familiar ritualized tirade. Each holiday,
as she puts up decorations, he says, "Didn't you
just do this?" or "Didn't we just take these down?"
She knows in a minute he may even start ranting
about The Nutcracker "making no goddamn sense,"
so she says, "You know what I like about holidays?"
He pauses, frowning, as if wondering what anyone
could possible like; she sips her drink then says,
"Most milestones? They only occur once, 16, 18, 21,
a baby's first word, proms, weddings, divorces,
the losses of those we love, but the holidays cycle,
so, as relieved as we may be when each one is done,
as ready as we are to wave goodbye to family,
we know next year we'll get a chance to do better.
Next year we won't get so annoyed. Next year,
we won't burn the cookies. We'll give better gifts.
We'll remember to buy fuses. We'll be people
that people want to be around. Next year we'll be
the people we want to be. Holidays are hope."
She raises a hand to stop him from responding.
"You whine and moan like holidays are millstones
on which we grind out our days. They're not.
They're cornerstones on which we build our lives."
She stands, as if embarrassed, and turns away
to refill their glasses, and he too is embarrassed,
recognizing how his complaining over the years
has been corroding something important to her.
Later he'll realize that she has given him a gift.
Later he'll begin to buy her an ornament each year,
the first one saying "Hope." For now, he mutters,
"Well, I don't know about millstones. I just don't
want to see a giant werewolf in Costco in August."

ACKNOWLEDGMENTS

Amaranth Journal: "Super Bowl Sunday"

Arboreal Literary Review: "Navigating a National Cemetery on Memorial Day"

As It Ought to Be: "Skeletons in the Waffle House" and "Because He's Still Recuperating His Partner Makes the Annual Happy Birthday Darwin! Cake" (as "The Scientist After the Operation")

Backchannels: "Home Alone"

bramble: "The Elf's Holiday" and "Ritual"

The Broadkill Review: "Autumn"

ChangeSeven: "Cycling"

Delta Poetry Review: "Education" and "Valentine"

Dodging the Rain: "Defender of the Faith" and "Home and the Holidays"

Eclectica Magazine: "The Gifts"

Fall Lines: "Those of Us with Bushy White Beards"

Flint Hills Review: "Event Horizon"

The Hong Kong Review: "What Love May Look Like"

Innisfree Poetry Journal: "Overheard at the Children's Museum"

Litbreak: "Flashing" and "Growth"

New Feathers Anthology: "Cakes" and "Ghosts"

One: "Souling" and "On the Way Home from the Civil Rights Museum My Fourteen-Year-Old Daughter Explains Why She Wants to Get a Tattoo"

One Art: "Nostalgia," "Party Planning in the Assisted Living Home" and "Veterans Day"

The Orchards Poetry Journal: "Snow Day"

Pinesong: "Democracy: Cake or Yeast"

Rattle: "Guttering"

Red Clay Review: "On Teaching My Son to Spell F-O-R-N-I-C-A-T-I-O-N and Other Conversations"

Red Eft Review: "What We Carry"

Salmon Creek Journal: "Monday Morning, Illuminated"

Salvation South: "Archaeology," "Marching Fourth" and "Spin"

Snapdragon Journal: "Call It Cake"

South Florida Poetry Journal: "Giblets" and "Winter Night, Music Lesson"

Streetlight: "Horses"

Stillwater Review: "Anniversary" (as "Journey")

Stirring: A Literary Collection: "Harvest Moon"

The Summerset Review: "What's Revealed" and "The Company We Keep"

Triggerfish Critical Review: "Mother's Day, 1961" and "How to Break Your Hand"

The 2 River View: "Accumulation" and "Buffet"

Wild Goose Poetry Review: "Braids" and "Lot's Wife"

Holiday Listing

January 1, New Year's Day: "New Year's Day"

Third Monday of January, Martin Luther King, Jr Day: "On the Way Home from the Civil Rights Museum My Fourteen-Year-Old Daughter Explains Why She Wants to Get a Tattoo"

February 2, Groundhog Day: "Groundhog Day"

First Sunday in February, Super Bowl Sunday: "Super Bowl Sunday"

February 12, National Darwin Day: "Because He's Still Recuperating His Partner Makes the Annual Happy Birthday Darwin! Cake"

February 14, Valentine's Day: "Valentine," "What Love May Look Like" and "What's Revealed"

February 22, National Margarita Day: "Checkpoints"

March 4, National Son Day: "Marching Fourth" and "Teaching My Son How to Spell F-O-R-N-I-C-A-T-I-O-N and Other Conversations

March 17, St. Patrick's Day: "Education"

Third Saturday in April, Record Store Day: "Archaeology"

May 4, Star Wars Day: "And Also with You"

May 18, International Museum Day: "Overheard at the Children's Museum"

Second Sunday in May, Mother's Day: "Mother's Day, 1961" and "Lot's Wife"

Last Monday in May, Memorial Day: "Navigating a National Cemetery on Memorial Day" and "Memory Machines, or Cutting the Grass on Memorial Day Weekend"

Bulky Item Day: "Cycling" and "Spin"

First Friday of June, National Donut Day: "Democracy: Cake or Yeast"

June 12, Loving Day: "Loving Day"

Third Sunday in June, Father's Day: "Cleats"

Fourth of July: "What Apple Pie Tastes Like" and "Fireworks

July 9, National Deadhead Day: "Evening Song"

First Monday in September, Labor Day: "Monday Morning, Illuminated"

First Sunday in September after Labor Day, National Grandparents Day: "What I Understand Now"

Autumnal Equinox: "Harvest Moon"

September 22 or 23, First Day of Fall: "Autumn"

September 25, National Daughter Day: "Braids"

September 25, National Comic Book Day: "What We Carry"

The tenth day of the Jewish month of Tishrie, Yom Kippur: "*Season's Greetings!*"

October 31, Halloween: "Skeletons in the Waffle House," "Growth," "Souling" and "Ghosts"

November 11, Veterans Day: "Veterans Day"

Fourth Thursday in November, Thanksgiving: "The Company We Keep," "Traditions," "In My Kitchen, Depressed, I Think of Richard Feynman Dancing" and "Thanksgiving"

Day after Thanksgiving, Black Friday: "Black Friday"

December 13, National Horse Day: "Horses"

December 25, Christmas: "Accumulation" and "Nostalgia"

December 26, Boxing Day: "Boxes"

December 31, New Year's Eve: "Outing, New Year's Eve"

A professor at the University of North Carolina School of the Arts, Joseph Mills holds an endowed chair, the Susan Burress Wall Distinguished Professorship in the Humanities. He has published eight collections of poetry with Press 53. His book *This Miraculous Turning* was awarded the 2015 Roanoke-Chowan Award for Poetry, and his collection *Angels, Thieves, and Winemakers* was called "a must have for wine lovers" by the *Washington Post*. His poetry has been featured several times on Garrison Keillor's *The Writer's Almanac* and in former U.S. poet laureate Ted Kooser's nationally syndicated newspaper column "American Life in Poetry." In addition to his volumes of poetry, he has researched and written two editions of *A Guide to North Carolina's Wineries* with his wife, Danielle Tarmey. He also has edited a collection of film criticism, *A Century of the Marx Brothers*. He has degrees in literature from the University of Chicago, the University of New Mexico, and the University of California, Davis.